Overcoming Objections

Making Network Marketing Rejection-Free

KEITH & TOM "BIG AL" SCHREITER

Published by Fortune Network Publishing

PO Box 890084

Houston, TX 77289 USA

+1 (281) 280-9800

BigAlBooks.com

Print ISBN: 978-1-956171-06-8

Ebook ISBN: 978-1-956171-07-5

CONTENTS

PREFACE.

Objections happen.

How we react to objections makes a difference in how we enjoy our careers as network marketers. React? Yes. And we have two choices.

Choice #1: Objections! Oh my! My prospects hate me. This is so negative. I will fail again.

Choice #2: Only interested prospects have objections. Their objections are questions they want answered. Maybe they are pointing out areas where they need to know more. They want what I have to offer, but need a bit more input and assurance from me.

So ... which choice will we take?

Objections are not a live/die, win/lose, fight-to-the-death verbal combat. Objections highlight what bothers our prospects. This is our chance to help.

MAKING ENEMIES WHEREVER WE GO.

---

1. Objections happen.
2. So we talk.
3. No one listens.

That formula doesn't work.

Yet, this is the formula most people use when handling objections.

When I started network marketing, I thought handling objections meant showing prospects they were wrong, and getting them to see things my way. I was in for a rude surprise.

My original strategy?

Argue.

Yes, I would disagree with prospects who would dig in their heels, feel insulted, and leave our argument even more convinced they were right. That's failure in so many ways.

Here is an over-exaggerated example of my original objection routine.

Prospect: "Too expensive. I can't afford it."

Me: "Yes you can afford it."

Prospect: "No I can't afford it. I am paying lots of credit card debt now, and my mortgage is overdue. My wife and I have a tight budget."

Me: "You can cut back on some expenses, I am sure. Food is overrated. This is a great opportunity."

Prospect: "I don't think so. I don't have any money to spare."

Me: "That is exactly why you should do this."

Prospect: "Stop your agenda. I know you want to earn a commission off me. But I have to think of my family first."

Me: "Well, uh … uh …"

• • •

This method didn't work. My lack of results proved that disagreeing with prospects was the express route to a communication failure.

Can we browbeat our prospects into logical submission? No.

Can we flood our prospects with facts proving that our point of view is right, and hope they change? No.

Instead, let's not fear objections. People aren't mean. They just report what they have experienced to date. Make their experience with us change their attitude about network marketing.

Easy to say. But how do we take action?

This is what we can do.

The first rule for objections is to agree.

If we talk, and our prospects resist, we will watch our words bounce off their foreheads and trickle down to the floor. Communication requires an open mind with our listeners.

When we disagree with our prospects, what happens?

First, do we trust and like people who disagree with us? No. So our prospects won't like it either. Making enemies is a bad strategic plan.

Second, our human minds can only hold one little thought at a time. Unfortunately, prospects won't want to entertain our thought. They prefer their thoughts. So while we are telling prospects all the reasons they are wrong, what are they thinking? They are dreaming up new "facts" to support their position when it is their turn to talk.

The final result?

- Our prospects don't listen to what we say.
- Our prospects don't like us.
- Our prospects think up even more reasons not to accept our offer.
- We created a lose-lose situation.

This is not the path we want to take.

Our new plan?

Respect our prospects. Their objections are real for them. Yes, they may not understand everything, or have the same life experiences we have. But we should feel that our prospects have good reasons for their objections.

And what will we do?

Agree.

We can agree their point of view has merit. That will be a good start.

What reaction can we expect from our prospects when we agree with their objections?

- Shock. (No high-pressure sales tactics approaching.)
- Joy. (I don't have to argue.)
- Trust. (You can see things from my point of view.)

When we agree, more good things happen. For us, we remove our fear of rejection. Now our prospects see us as friends or trusted consultants. We can now move forward with our discussion.

The first step?

To agree.

If we get this first step right, to agree, everything else gets easy.

So, if we are not a reader, only a skimmer of books, relax. Even if we read no further, if we take this one little step, to agree, we will be far ahead of all the pushy salesmen in the world.

Agree. It works.

HOW CAN I AGREE?

We must start with agreement. If we disagree, it is over. We would be talking, but no one would be listening.

Which words should I use to ease the tension after an objection? Start with:

- "Relax."
- "Exactly."
- "I see where you are coming from."
- "Makes sense."
- "It's okay."
- "Precisely."
- "Right."
- "So true."
- "Of course."
- "Yes, I see."
- "Correct."
- "Absolutely."

These starter words will relax our prospects and create open minds for our message.

Let's do some examples of using these words in our replies to objections.

- "Relax. This is only one more option for your life. It is okay to not take advantage of this extra income."
- "Makes sense. I would be careful also."
- "So true. We have to be careful what we spend our money on."
- "Yes, I see. There are only twenty-four hours in a day."
- "I see where you are coming from. I had those same thoughts also."
- "Right. We should always look at the pros and cons."

After making their objections, our prospects will react to our first few words. This is why agreement is so important in our first few words. Agreement puts our prospects at ease. They lower their defenses. Now they have open minds to hear our message.

We don't always have to start with these words, but we get the idea. We want to be a consultant, not an adversary when we hear objections. We and our prospects want the same thing: a better future.

Now, let's warm up our "objection muscles" with some easy objections. Then, we will move on to the next level, how to transcend this whole conversation. But first, let's practice a few common objections.

REMOVING THE "WHAT IF I FAIL?" OBJECTION.

We finish our presentation. Our prospects take a deep breath and say, "Sounds good. I could join and talk to my friends. But what if they don't buy or join? They will make fun of me. I will fail. And they will tease me and say, 'We told you so!'"

Our prospects might not say this, but they are thinking this! Everyone wants to avoid embarrassment in front of family and friends.

My worthless sponsor's advice? To say this:

"No pain, no gain! Don't think like a loser. Only weak people give up before they start. Get out of your victim mode. Don't make me vomit with your baby excuses."

Yeah. That is one way. That route won't get us far though. Prospects don't like to be told they are weak losers who allow life to beat them down. Maybe this type of caustic response is a qualifying requirement to be a worthless sponsor.

So instead, let's be more diplomatic.

Let's use words that won't endanger our lives.

First, we will remove rejection. We can say, "Relax. We don't have to sell or convince family and friends. Many will want what we have to offer, many won't. They know what is going on in their lives. We only gift them with one more option. It is up to them if they want what we offer now, or not. We don't want to feel bad by hiding this option from them."

Now our prospects realize there is no rejection. And if we don't pressure our friends, they won't retaliate and tease us later.

Second, let's tell our prospects that friends and relatives will only make up 0.01% of our sales in years to come. Whether they buy or join, or not, it won't affect our long-term business. Sales leaders report that most of their sales volume comes from people they didn't know when they started.

Third, let's not build a huge, successful business, and tell our friends about it later. That is disrespectful to our long-time friends. They don't have to join, but we never want them to say, "Why did you keep this a secret from me?" Now that would be embarrassing.

"I don't think I can succeed in this business."

Here is one way to reply to this common objection.

"I understand. And yes, there is a risk when starting something new, but I will be your partner. Now, I have experience on what we need to do and have succeeded. I don't intend to fail now. So don't you think the two of us have a pretty good chance of making your new business work?"

What will our prospects think? "Well, I will try hard. But my sponsor knows how to do this, and will be my partner. Together we should be okay and succeed."

When our new team members start with confidence, and a positive expectation of impending success, they will get positive reactions from their prospects. Prospects can sense confidence.

Or, we can try another approach.

To this objection we can say, "Of course you don't know how to work this business. The company doesn't expect you to know how to build a business before you join. That would be insane. That is why the company provides training after you join, so you can learn how to build your business effectively."

This answer assures our prospects that it is okay to fear the future, but this answer isn't as powerful as when we offer to partner with them.

"But, but ... I don't know what to say!"

Again, we will start with agreement. Disagreement tells our prospects they were wrong. They hate that. So, we will initially agree with their objections. Why? Because their objections make perfect sense to them right now, from their point of view. We need to respect that.

But here is an easy answer.

"Well, of course you don't know what to say to people. (Remember, agreement early.) The company doesn't expect you to know what to say before you start. So relax. You haven't learned any skills for our business yet, but you will learn these skills over the next several months. You and I could learn to do anything in an hour a day over time, right? We could even learn to play the piano by practicing an hour a day over time."

"This is too risky for me."

Do we know any conservative people? People who never want to take a chance? People who want all the stoplights to be green before they leave on a trip?

The uncertainty of having one's own business scares them. But here is something fun to do. We can use their fear of risk to motivate them to join. Let's see how that works with this answer for this objection.

"You are so right. We shouldn't take risks. Having all of our income from only one source, our job, is very risky. It is a good idea to have a part-time business on the side. This way we don't put all of our future in the hands of a company or a boss."

"I don't have any money!"

Well, that is a common objection. Could this be true?

Yes!

Our prospect says, "I don't have any money! I'm living on Mars, lost my wallet and they blocked my internet banking."

Well, that would be true. No money.

But what about prospects who don't fall into this category? The prospects who have money, access to money, or don't think they should spend their money to start a business of their own?

First, we agree. Then we put these prospects into a position where they must make a choice for their lives. Remember, they must make the choices for themselves. All we do is offer them one more option for their lives.

How would our answer to the "No money!" objection sound?

"I agree. You probably don't have extra spare cash, just waiting for an opportunity. After all, everyone has expenses, right? We spend our money on clothes, pizzas, restaurants, Internet packages, mobile phones, haircuts, manicures, beer, movies and more. There is only so much money to go around. The real question is what we decide to spend our money on. For some, movies to relax are more important than having their own business. For others, having their own business is more important than a few haircuts. It is always a choice."

"But I need a job and paycheck now, not a part-time business."

"Absolutely. The most important thing you can do is to get that next job. Now, between interviews, sending resumes, and waiting for the phone to ring, here is what we can do. Let's not waste these weeks and months waiting for that job offer. While waiting for the phone to ring, we can start building your part-time business. Then, if you are out of work again, you will have a second income to make things easier."

What about objections from our team members?

Yes, we must learn to handle them also. Let's take a look at a common team member objection.

"NOBODY WILL GIVE ME REFERRALS."

"Help me! Help me!"

Our new team member whines, "I can't build this business. Nobody will give me referrals. Everyone tells me they don't know anyone. They claim they moved and haven't met their neighbors. They lost their Christmas card list. Every time I beg for referrals, they balk. How do I handle this rejection?"

This is discouraging. We believe in what we offer, yet our prospects don't believe in us or our offer. They refuse to recommend us to others. Prospects don't want to unleash a salesman on their friends, and then lose that future friendship.

So let's look at the two biggest objections we will have to overcome.

#1. "I don't believe your offer."

Prospects make this judgment before they know our wonderful benefits and facts. Before our countless testimonials. Before our company video.

What can we do to manage this snap decision by our prospects?

Two words.

"Most people."

When we say the words "most people" in conversation, prospects immediately place themselves in the "most people" group. Humans have a survival program that says, "Stay with the group. Be safe. Don't take chances. Don't be a loner." This mental program activates instantly.

This helps prospects think, "Hmmm, I am part of most people. I do what most people do. I believe what most people believe. And I am sure I will believe what you say next as I know I already believe it."

This is a good start to overcoming our prospects' skepticism.

#2. "I am afraid you will force me to buy or do something."

This is a real fear. We will remove this fear by telling our prospects, "Hey, this is just another option for you. It is up to you if you want this option or not."

Wow! Their fears melt away. No one will pressure them. They get to choose. They are in control.

We also reposition ourselves in the eyes of our prospects. Now we don't look or seem to be a salesman. They feel that we are more of a friend or a consultant trying to help them.

Gifting people another option in their lives? Magic.

Now, let's put these ideas to work.

Not only are we going to get referrals from our soon-to-be customers, but we will also get referrals from them, even if they don't become a customer. Seems hard to imagine? Let's do it.

Imagine we sold discounted electricity. To our prospects, we say:

"Most people who use our service save a lot on their electricity bill. And, they want to keep their friends and relatives from overpaying also. Now, you may or may not want to save money with us. That is up to you. But could you do me a favor? Whether you decide to save money with us or not, would you at least let your friends and relatives know that they can save a lot of money on their electric bill too?"

A lot happens in these six sentences. It happens so fast, the results are automatic. No thinking involved.

Time to break down the magic. Ready?

Us: "Most people who use our service save a lot on their electricity bill."

Prospects think, "Well if most people save a lot of money, it must be true. No more facts or proof needed. The service can save me money."

Us: "And, they want to keep their friends and relatives from overpaying also."

Prospects think: "So true. My friends are good people. I want to help the people I know. I am not a selfish jerk. Of course, I want to keep my friends and relatives from overpaying. Especially my mom!"

Us: "Now, you may or may not want to save money with us."

Prospects think: "You read my mind! You have superpowers I can only aspire to. I trust you. We think the same. You seem okay with me choosing what is best for me. I guess you are not a salesman after all."

Us: "That is up to you."

Prospects think: "Great. I am in control. No one is trying to manipulate or push me in a corner. I can relax."

Us: "But could you do me a favor?"

Prospects think: "Sure. You just left me 'off the hook' and I appreciate that. So a favor? No problem. Happy to do it."

Us: "Whether you decide to save money with us or not, would you at least let your friends and relatives know they can save a lot of money on their electric bill too?"

Prospects think, "Sure. I am like most people. So I will want to be your customer and save money on my electricity bill. Makes sense. And I'm happy to let my friends benefit also. And even if there is some reason I can't be your customer now, I will still let others know."

Things are looking good.

Our prospects feel relaxed.

- No sales pressure.
- Our prospects want to be a customer.
- We don't feel like a pushy salesman.
- We improved our chances of getting referrals.

Now for some examples of other products or services. We will use the same template.

"Most people who use our identity theft protection service, love the 24-hour coverage. They sleep well at night, knowing their credit cards, bank accounts, and even their credit histories are safe from criminal tampering. And, they want to make sure their friends and relatives get the same protection also. Now, you may or may not want to protect yourself from cybercrime with us. That is up to you. But could you do me a favor? Whether you decide to protect your money, credit and reputation with us or not, would you at least let your friends and relatives know they can get our full protection?"

For vitamins?

"Most people who use our vitamins feel younger in only a few days. And, they want to keep their friends and relatives from feeling old also. Now, you may or may not want to feel younger and more energetic with us. That is up to you. But could you do me a favor? Whether you decide to feel better with us or not, would you at least let your friends and relatives know they can start feeling like they are 16 years old again, but with better judgment?"

Skincare?

"Most people love how our night moisturizer makes their skin younger while they sleep. And, they want to help their friends and relatives look younger also. Now, you may or may not want to start looking younger with us. That is up to you. But could you do me a favor? Whether you decide to look younger with us or not, would you at least let your friends and relatives know they can start looking younger while they sleep? So they can make their older-looking friends jealous?" (Okay, a little harsh when not talking to a good friend, but we can edit as needed.)

We get the idea. Pretty simple to adjust for the products or services we offer.

But what about our business opportunity? Yes, we could use the same template.

"Most people who see our part-time business get excited about it and want to earn extra money. And, they want their friends and relatives to have a look at this opportunity also. Now, you may or may not want to earn extra money with us. That is up to you. But could you do me a favor? Whether you decide to earn extra money with us or not, would you at least let your friends and relatives know they can have extra money to help them every month?"

What if we offered travel? A bonus car? Weekly payouts? No problem. With a little creativity, this template can work.

Referrals get easier when we make it more comfortable for our prospects. Because we use no sales pressure, this template makes us feel better too.

When our team members complain they have no prospects, this is a great solution. They can now get referrals from prospects, even if the prospects don't take the offer themselves.

Let's move on to more common objections from our prospects.

"THAT IS WHY I AM TALKING TO YOU NOW."

This objection template is an easy way to fill in the blanks. We could answer almost any objection with this template. The warning though is this: we must say this with sincerity and not in a manipulative way.

The examples that follow are the bare bones outline. We will want to add some cushion words or phrases and make these examples feel more personal.

"I don't have any money."

"Of course you don't have any money. That is why I am talking to you now. You don't want to be that way for the rest of your life. So let's sit down now and figure out a way for you to start, so you finally can get the money you want."

"I don't have any time."

"Of course you don't have any time. That is why I am talking to you now. You don't want to be that way for the rest of your life, never having any time to call your own. So let's sit down now and figure out a way to get your business started in the few minutes you have every day, so that you will eventually have enough money to get some free time in your life."

"I don't know anybody."

"Of course you don't know anybody. That is why I am talking to you now. You don't want to be that way for the rest of your life. So let's get started now and join the company training program that teaches how to meet great prospects every day. It is something we can learn, and we will build a great business together."

This template is simple and can be applied to many common objections we encounter.

Need an easier template?

What can we say immediately after our prospects' objection?

"Let's talk about that."

That diffuses the win/lose or live/die feeling of directly answering the objection. We can lower the tension by asking further details. Sometimes we get surprised as our prospects meant something different in their objections than what we assumed.

So in a pinch, when we can't think of anything to say, let's answer, "Let's talk about that."

"I DON'T HAVE ANYONE TO TALK TO."

Our frustrated team member complains to us. "I don't know anybody. Nobody wants to talk to me. I am afraid of strangers. I don't know what to say! I am not social. I don't have time to meet new people and build a relationship."

As leaders, we hear this objection a lot. As humans, we love to blame outside circumstances for our failures. It is never our fault. But with a little creativity, we can make this worse. We can impose unrealistic restrictions that make it impossible to succeed.

One distributor messaged me this. "I only leave my house to go to church. I don't want to talk about my business there. Since I never meet anyone, and don't know anyone, and hate social media, I can't build my business. So what are you going to do about it?"

Nice.

When team members place unrealistic restrictions on what they will do to succeed, it is time to take a hint. They may be looking for a way to exit their business and save face. They don't want their failure to be their fault.

But what if our team members are sincere? What if there is a hint of actually wanting to talk to prospects?

In that case, let's give our team members something that works. If the words we give get results, the objection goes away.

What are the words?

Not these words.

"Do you know anyone that would be interested?"

Those words guarantee this response, "Nope. Can't think of anyone."

This request is too general. Most people will respond that they don't know anyone.

Instead, let's recommend these words.

"I am looking for people with this problem, who want to fix it. Do you know anyone like that?"

These words can give presold prospects for our frustrated team members. The prospect thinks, "Yeah. I know several people with that problem. My friend, Joe, has that problem. And oh my! He desperately wants to fix his problem." And now the prospect feels good about recommending his friend, Joe.

The best news is that so many people have problems, our prospecting gets easy.

Some examples of this script?

I am looking for stressed people who need a vacation, and need some extra money to afford it.

I am looking for college students with student loans, who want a plan on how to get them paid off.

I am looking for underpaid secretaries who want to supplement their office salaries."

I am looking for crazy people who want to change their careers to something more interesting.

I am looking for people over 50 who don't have pensions, and want to have extra money when they retire.

I am looking for sales clerks who hate standing on their feet all day, and want to have a different career.

I am looking for social people who love coffee breaks and chatting with people, and would love to have a career of taking five coffee breaks a day.

Could we be a bit more aggressive? Certainly. Of course we have to use our judgment though. A female networker wrote me, "I sell skin care and nutrition, but I can't seem to get other women interested. What could I say that would light up their imagination?"

Using our judgment, here are some more aggressive examples.

I am looking for women who have wrinkles, and don't want to bring them to their class reunion.

I am looking for women with stretch marks, and don't want them.

I am looking for women who can't sleep at night because they hear their skin wrinkling.

I am looking for women who don't want to end up with skin looking like a prune.

I am looking for mothers of the bride with extra weight, who don't want to dominate the pictures.

Okay, maybe we went too far, but we get the idea. The more emotional the problem, the more people will want to fix the problem.

And finally, to all these statements we add the question, "Do you know anyone like that?"

This is an easy conversation with strangers. We don't ask strangers to buy or join. Of course, if the strangers had the problem we mentioned, and wanted to fix the problem, we could have instant prospects.

This little script is a good solution to the "I have no prospects" objection.

My favorite statement to get great prospects?

If you read other Big Al books, this might sound familiar.

"I am looking for people with two jobs, who would like to get rid of one of those jobs."

What do we know about people with two jobs? Well, they need extra money. That is why they are working. They are self-starters. They went out and got that extra job. Do they want to work two jobs for the rest of their lives? Of course not. If we could help them get rid of one of their jobs, they would be thrilled. We could expect a big hug. And if we could help them get rid of both of their jobs, they might hug us so hard it would crush our ribs.

This little prospecting script can point us towards the best, most open-minded prospects other people know. So if we have a choice of who to talk to, let's talk to the most qualified people we can.

People have problems, and we have solutions.

When our team members have objections, maybe they are not trying to be negative. Maybe they don't know a solution. That is why we should have great objection skills to pass on as sponsors.

Let's get back to some common objections from our prospects now.

"IT'S A PYRAMID!"

Gasp! Choke! Uh, uh … what will we do next?

Our prospects accuse us of operating an illegal scheme, stealing from others, and look at us as if we are criminals on the run.

What should we do? Here is a short answer.

We have to say something. Silence confirms our prospects' evil suspicions, but what can we say? In our book, *How to Prospect, Sell and Build Your Network Marketing Business with Stories*, we tell of Robert Butwin's short answer. This is easy for new team members to learn. Plus, it reinforces their belief in network marketing. Here is the story.

• • •

"Before I answer your question, is it okay if I ask you a question?

"When you were getting your formal education at school, if your teachers would have received a small percentage of your earnings for the rest of your life, do you think your formal education would have been better?"

The prospect answers, "Of course."

Robert continues, "Well, that is how network marketing works. Your sponsor wants to teach and train you to be as successful as possible, because the only way your sponsor can earn money is by making you successful."

• • •

With this simple, short story, we replace the objection with a benefit. This answer is intellectually satisfying, but may not be enough for overcoming our prospects' biases.

We can do much better as professionals.

Where do objections come from?

We cause them!

Uh-oh. Personal responsibility approaching. We hate personal responsibility, but let's get on with it.

People don't use their free will. We spend most of our time reacting. Think of how many decisions we have to make in one second:

- Left foot, then my right foot.
- Remember to breathe.
- Time for my heart to beat again.
- Pump blood to the brain. Hurry!
- Scratch that itch.
- Create 30,000 new digestive enzymes.
- Send a few killer T-cells over there.

Okay, there are way too many decisions for our minds to think through. Our conscious minds can only have one thought at a time. So instead of using our free will, we make 99.9% of our decisions automatically, reacting to whatever happens. Some examples?

- Someone says "Hi" and we instinctively reply "Hi" back.
- Someone says "Thank you" and we reply "You are welcome" as a habit.

- We hear a loud noise and freeze.
- The sun gets a bit hot and we sweat.
- Someone frowns at us and our emotions take over.

We can't think through everything. Not enough time. So what is our only alternative? To react automatically to what others say or do.

And that brings us to this embarrassing question, "If prospects react to what we say, then who really creates objections?"

Guess that would be … us.

Want a great example? This adventure shows us how we create our own objections.

"How to ruin a meal with leaders."

I am in Belgium to do a Big Al workshop on how to close our prospects. Before the workshop, 12 leaders and I went for a nice evening dinner. Plenty of time. Everything seems to start later in Belgium.

The food? Excellent. I was enjoying my meal when the lady on my left interrupted my calorie shoveling by asking, "So how do you handle the pyramid objection?"

I thought, "I could pretend not to hear her so I can continue eating uninterrupted. But that would be rude. I better answer. Maybe I could say something short, and then get back to my second helping of mashed potatoes."

I smiled at her and said, "Well, it happens sometimes. Don't worry about it."

Back to eating.

She continued, "It happens all the time. Every time. So how do we handle the pyramid objection?"

Groan. This wasn't going away. The mashed potatoes were waiting. I tried one more stall tactic. "Well, possibly it was some bad prospects."

She wasn't buying my stall tactics. She upped her game. She got everyone's attention, and asked her fellow leaders, "So how many of us get the pyramid objection all the time?"

Unanimous. The other leaders smiled in approval. They stared at me. She turned to me and asked again, "So how should we handle the pyramid objection? Everyone here gets it all the time. What should we say?"

I stalled.

I said, "Let's see what we are using now."

Then, I asked my "challenging lady" on my left, "So when you get the pyramid objection, what do you say now?"

Her quick reply, "I tell them we are a legitimate company. We belong to associations. Our strong code of ethics ensures that we have the best interests of our customers at heart."

Hmmm. I then asked, "How is that working?"

"Not at all. They still say it is a pyramid and they don't want to join."

Next, I turned to the man on my right. I asked him, "So when you get the pyramid objection, what do you say?"

"I tell them the government is a pyramid. The prime minister on top, and then the different levels of government below. We are like the government."

Hmmm. I asked him, "How is that working?"

"It doesn't work. They are still not convinced. They don't join."

I asked the next man on the right, "So when you get the pyramid objection, what do you say now?"

"I insist that all companies are pyramids. The chairman of the board is on top. The board directors next. Then management. And finally, the workers at the bottom."

Hmmm. I asked him, "So how is that working for you?"

"It isn't working."

After a few more of the same answers, I said, "We all know people are reactive, right? So what is it that everyone here is doing or saying that gets prospects to react with the pyramid objection?"

Dead silence.

Many people looked down at their food. Some moved their eyes back and forth to see if anyone would answer.

More silence. Sort of like a high-tension horror movie.

No one was going to talk. Everyone seemed to know the answer, but no one dared to be the first person to let me in on their insider secret.

I looked at my mashed potatoes growing cold. I didn't feel now was an appropriate time to resume shoveling calories. And so, I waited.

The tension finally got so high that one man across the table swallowed hard and spoke up. He dropped the bombshell.

"Our company has a specific presentation they train us to do. Everyone uses this presentation. We call it the 'cocktail napkin' presentation. To explain how to grow our business, we grab a small square paper cocktail napkin, the kind we see at bars. Then, we draw a circle at the top. We write the word 'you' inside of the circle.

Next, we draw two lines down from the 'you' circle and attach two new circles to represent their first two team members. Looks like a triangle now ..."

Uh-oh. I get it.

To present their company's compensation plan, their graphic is ... oh my!

I asked the group, "If we don't want prospects to say we are a pyramid, then why do we draw a picture of a pyramid?"

The rest of the meal felt quiet and subdued. I finally got a chance to finish those mashed potatoes.

In the workshop following our evening meal, we discussed, "Why we shouldn't draw pyramids when presenting to prospects."

We cause it!

Often network marketing leaders pronounce, "I never get the pyramid objection!" Now we know why. When we say and do something different, prospects react to us.

Q. So what is the best way to avoid the pyramid objection?

A. Don't cause it. Change what we say and do.

Still don't believe we cause the pyramid objection?

We never see a random stranger walk down the street, slap his forehead and spontaneously yell out, "It is a pyramid!"

Nope. Doesn't happen.

Prospects react to what we say and do.

Yes, something we say or do will trigger the pyramid objection. Our job is to mentally backtrack to see what we did.

"I WANT TO THINK IT OVER."

Prospect: "I need to think it over."

Networker: "Oh, okay. Until when?"

Prospect: "Until the holidays."

Networker: "Which holidays?"

Prospect: "Christmas 2067."

Networker: "Should I call you then, or will you call me?"

Prospect: "I will call you."

Networker: "Great. I will schedule this in my diary. Will wait for your call."

The dreaded "I want to think it over" objection plagues us until we learn the simple skills to fix this delay tactic. And if we haven't heard the "I want to think it over" version, maybe these versions will sound more familiar.

- "I need to research this more."
- "I am not sure my job allows me to do what I want on my time off."
- "I have to check with my spouse first."
- "Let me sleep on this."

- "Let me run it by my friends tomorrow and let them make decisions for my life."

Okay, a little exaggerated, but the delay is real.

Reality?

There is always a decision. Every time. Always.

Our prospects either make a decision to:

1. Accept our offer, or

2. To keep their lives the same.

There is no maybe.

"Not making a decision ... is making a decision not to do it."

What happens when we delay making a decision? We are making a decision to keep our circumstances the same.

Here are a few examples.

Example #1. We are standing at the cruise ship port, waiting for our dream cruise to leave. They announce, "Final boarding." Now, if we want to wait and think it over for 15 minutes, what happens? Our cruise ship leaves without us! Not making a decision to board now is a decision to stay where we are. Not making a decision was a decision to miss our dream cruise. We don't want life to make choices for us. We want to be in control.

Example #2. We are standing in the middle of a busy expressway. Cars and trucks speed towards us. We think to ourselves, "Do I run to the right, or do I run to the left?" But we decided to think about it for a while. What happens? Smash! By delaying and not making a decision to move either right or left, we made a decision to become a human speed bump for the oncoming traffic. Ouch.

Example #3. There is a one-day sale at our favorite department store. We think, "Should I rush down for the big sale, or should I continue to relax with my pizza and watch my favorite shows?" We think about it some more. Getting a babysitter, driving through traffic, finding parking … but the reward is huge discounts on our favorite clothes. We watch another episode of our favorite show. And then another. And soon, it is too late to arrange a trip to our favorite department store. We made the decision by default.

A decision to delay and think it over is … a decision to keep our current situation.

That means delaying the decision, thinking it over, is another way of giving us a "No" decision. Will prospects change their minds in the future? Possible, but not likely.

Prospects use the "I need to think it over" decision for many reasons.

Some examples?

1. To get rid of us. They don't want to argue or defend their "No" decision. They want to escape.

2. To be social. Our friends don't want to reject us and tell us "No" to our face. Bad manners. Definitely not polite. Instead, they want to let us down gently and delay the pain of giving us their "No" decision. In a way, we should appreciate our friends helping us to save face.

3. They don't understand what we offer. The human reaction is, "When in doubt, the answer is a 'No' decision."

4. The big reason. Change is risky. Accepting our offer means a new and dangerous change in our prospects' lives. Let's look at this "risky" program now.

"Breathe. Stay safe. Don't move. Avoid taking a chance."

This program runs full-time in the human brain. And yes, we have the same program as our prospects. Delaying decisions feels safer.

This is normal. As professionals, we need to expect our prospects to react to decisions by hesitating.

Let's see how humans get this program to delay decisions.

First, think back in time. Have we ever made a bad decision? Of course. Now, how did we feel about that bad decision? We felt bad. Really bad. We felt loss and embarrassment. Later, when we thought about that decision again, yes, we felt just as bad. We do this over and over. Bad decisions are hard to forget.

So what happens in our minds? Our subconscious minds feel that we repeated this bad decision hundreds or even thousands of times. How does our subconscious mind react?

It creates a program that tells us, "Don't make any more decisions. Delay decisions as long as possible. We don't want the trauma and drama of another bad decision. Let's hope something happens to make the decision for us as we don't want to be responsible for a bad decision."

As we see, the objection, "I want to think it over," is normal. We programmed our minds to avoid decisions at all costs.

It gets worse. It isn't entirely our fault. Why?

Because other people program our minds to avoid decisions also. Think about jobs. Does our boss say to us, "Please make your own decisions on what to do. There is no need to follow our company policies and instructions."

Ha. Ha. That doesn't happen. Employers insist that the employees follow instructions precisely. We don't get a reward for making independent decisions. However, we can get severe penalties for making independent decisions. Yes, jobs program us to never make decisions.

Now that we understand that delaying decisions is normal, we won't panic when we get that objection.

Instead, let's learn how to handle the "I want to think it over" objection professionally.

Ready?

"MY PROSPECT USED TO BE INDECISIVE. NOW HE IS NOT SURE."

Okay, it isn't this bad, but prospects love to hide behind the "I want to think it over" objection. They feel safer when they don't take a chance or make a change.

As we learned earlier, to answer objections, we should start with agreement. This is to keep our prospect's minds open so they hear what we say.

Agreement is easy if we practice empathy. Try looking at this objection from our prospects' viewpoint. We don't know the background of our prospects. We don't know what happened to them before we talked to them today. And we don't know the drama and trauma in their lives.

This helps us to be more forgiving when we hear objections.

So let's build a simple template for this objection now. Our first words will be the most important.

Prospects judge us immediately.

Earlier in this book, we showed a formula for saying "Relax"

"Relax. It is okay."

When we say these words, how will our prospects feel?

A deep sigh of relief. No need to defend the objection. Our prospects won't fear what we say next. The advantages of these four words? Our prospects:

- Feel relaxed.
- Like us because we listened to them.
- We keep good trust and rapport.
- Our prospects want to hear what we say next.

Things are looking up already.

Don't fight our prospects' survival program.

Remember, this program has lived inside of our prospects since birth. We can't expect to change it with a few words. Instead, we will get our prospects to focus on a simple truth.

"Not making a decision ... is making a decision not to do it."

Delaying a decision is a decision for keeping our lives the same.

How do we do this?

We will describe the results of not accepting our offer. Yes, letting our prospects keep their problems will be uncomfortable for them. And now they realize a choice is imminent. We removed the luxury of our prospects thinking, "If I delay, I won't be making a decision. I will be safe." Now, they must choose.

Let's add to our first four words. Ready for some examples?

- "Relax, it is okay to continue getting by on one paycheck."

- "Relax, it is okay to continue commuting in that freeway traffic every day."
- "Relax, it is okay to continue with the sleepless nights."
- "Relax, it is okay to wait and see if you will get a raise next year at work."
- "Relax, it is okay to not use this stem cell moisturizer."
- "Relax, it is okay to keep paying the higher electricity rates."
- "Relax, it is okay to pay for your family's vacations out of savings."
- "Relax, it is okay to make a decision to leave your family uninsured today."
- "Relax, it is okay to make a decision to wait until age 67 for retirement."
- "Relax, it is okay to make a decision not to start a side income now."

So instead of arguing with our prospects, let's agree. Let's tell our undecided prospects that it is okay to lose out and miss their chance at our wonderful offer.

Our prospects feel respected. No need for rejection. So far, so good.

But it gets better.

Why?

Because every decision has consequences. And shouldn't we point out the negative consequences of not taking our offer? I think so.

At this point, we will remind our prospects of their problems. Not taking our offer means they will have to continue to live with their uncomfortable problems. So let's enhance our original statements.

- "Relax, it is okay to continue getting by on one paycheck and to continue to deal with the credit card debt."
- "Relax, it is okay to continue commuting in that freeway traffic every day. I know it will be frustrating to leave your home that early in the morning."
- "Relax, it is okay to continue with the sleepless nights. Many people have sleepless nights. It is possible to live with that tired feeling during the day."
- "Relax, it is okay to wait and see if you will get a raise next year at work. Let's hope that grocery prices don't go up in the meantime."
- "Relax, it is okay to not use this stem cell moisturizer. We can choose to let our skin age at its normal rate."
- "Relax, it is okay to keep paying the higher electricity rates, instead of using the savings to take the family out to eat more often."
- "Relax, it is okay to pay for your family's vacations out of savings, instead of earning a free vacation. Most people set aside extra money every month from their paycheck to fund it."
- "Relax, it is okay to make a decision to leave your family uninsured today. I know the stress of worrying makes it difficult to sleep."
- "Relax, it is okay to make a decision to wait until age 67 for retirement. That is only 23 years away."

- "Relax, it is okay to make a decision not to start a side income now. Let's hope prices for things go lower in the future."

How can we take this to an even higher level? With benefits.

Now we have open communication with our prospects. This gives us another opportunity to review the benefits of doing business with us. At this point, we will remind them of the benefits of making a decision to move forward with our offer.

Our conversation will now sound like this:

- "Relax, it is okay to continue getting by on one paycheck and to continue to deal with the credit card debt. But, it is also okay to get started tonight, so next month will be easier to manage."

- "Relax, it is okay to continue commuting in that freeway traffic every day. I know it will be frustrating to leave your home that early in the morning. But, it is also okay to start now so next year you can finally work at home."

- "Relax, it is okay to continue with the sleepless nights. Many people have sleepless nights. It is possible to live with that tired feeling during the day. But, it is also okay to start using our sleep product to change how you sleep and feel now."

- "Relax, it is okay to wait and see if you will get a raise next year at work. Let's hope that grocery prices don't go up in the meantime. But, it is also okay to start our part-time business now, while I have time to help you. Then you won't have to wait to see if the company will give raises next year."

- "Relax, it is okay not to use this stem cell moisturizer. We can choose to let our skin age at its normal rate. But it is also okay to start using this now, and look fabulous at your upcoming class reunion."

- "Relax, it is okay to keep paying the higher electricity rates, instead of using the savings to take the family out to eat more often. But, it is also okay to take five minutes now, and lower your rates immediately."

- "Relax, it is okay to pay for your family's vacations out of savings, instead of earning a free vacation. Most people set aside extra money every month from their paycheck to fund it. But, it is also okay to start your business now, and earn that dream vacation of a lifetime."

- "Relax, it is okay to make a decision to leave your family uninsured today. I know the stress of worrying makes it difficult to sleep. But, it is also okay to start the insurance immediately, and feel good that your family is protected."

- "Relax, it is okay to make a decision to wait until age 67 for retirement. That is only 23 years away. But, it is also okay to start now to build this part-time business so that you can retire years earlier."

- "Relax, it is okay to make a decision not to start a side income now. Let's hope prices for things go lower in the future. But, it is also okay to start this part-time business today, to future-proof yourself from inflation."

Let's review this objection technique.

#1. Agree with our prospects' "I want to think it over" objection. If we argue, our prospects won't be listening to us anyway. Instead, we will say, "Relax. It is okay." Prospects will always agree to relax, and feel great that it is okay to take our offer or not.

#2. Remove the luxury of procrastination from our prospects' minds. We point out that a decision must be made. There is no such thing as delaying. It is either to keep the circumstances the same or to take our offer.

#3. Point out the consequences of making a decision to keep circumstances the same. A little reminder of our prospects' problems helps.

#4. Point out the benefits of making the decision to act now. Tell the prospect, "But, it is also okay to make a decision to take action now." This reminds our prospects they must make a decision now.

And that is one way to take care of the "I need to think it over" objection.

But is this the only way?

Of course not. Let's look at more.

"YOU CAN SAY 'NO' TO OUR OFFER."

Prevention is better than fixing a problem after it happens. Here is a simple way to prevent the "I want to think it over" objection.

How?

Before we start our presentation or offer, we tell our prospects that they will be making a "Yes" or "No" decision. Now, we will do this politely, with no pressure, but the message gets through. Here is how we could deliver this message before we talk about our opportunity.

"I will tell you about our business, but when I do, please know that it is up to you. You can choose to keep your life the same. No problem. Or, you can choose to join our business, and work to earn that extra money you need."

What reaction can we expect from our prospects?

- They relax.
- They listen.
- They set aside their skepticism.
- And they know when we finish, they must decide.
- This tells our prospects they have two choices:
    1. "Yes."
    2. "No."

Can't get much simpler than this. This is a nice way to instruct prospects that we expect an immediate decision.

As an added benefit, think of how this makes it easier for prospects to listen with an open mind. They feel we have no agenda. We only want what is best for them. This feels great to them.

Now our prospects don't have to look for bad things in our offer. They know they won't need to justify a "No" decision to us.

Use the "choosing" word.

Instead of random oral diarrhea, let's choose better words to prompt our prospects into making immediate decisions. Here is the difference.

Amateur version: "Want to make up your mind now? Uh, what did you like best? Why not give it a try? Please?"

Not a powerful way to end a presentation. Plus, we act too late if we wait until the end. We will influence the immediate decision by choosing better words.

Professional version: "Choosing to move forward is a choice. Choosing not to move forward is also a choice."

Done. No more thinking it over or delaying tactics. The prospect has an opportunity to choose to move forward, or to choose not to take advantage of our offer.

How do our prospects feel about having control over their choices? Great! Relaxed. Empowered. Confident.

How do we feel when we direct our prospects to make a choice? Great! Relaxed. And we no longer worry about rejection.

With no sales pressure or fear, prospects can figure out what is best for them. And since our offers improve their lives, most will choose our option to move forward.

Let's do some examples of using the "choosing" word to get decisions.

- "Choosing to save money on our package vacation plans is a choice. But you can also choose to take your regular, more expensive vacation like last year."

- "Choosing to protect your identity from theft with us makes sense. But you can also choose to risk it, and hope it never happens."

- "Choosing to lose weight by having our diet shake for breakfast is easy. But you can also choose to struggle losing weight the old-fashioned way."

- "Choosing our miracle night moisturizer to stop wrinkling is a great option. But choosing to let nature have its way with our skin is a choice too."

- "Choosing to have a bullet-proof immune system is smart. But we could also choose to live unprotected."

Our prospects get to choose. However, we have the power of which options they have to choose from. Most prospects will make good decisions.

But what about some examples for our opportunity?

Use our imagination. Here are a few to get us started.

- "Choosing to take the first step to become your own boss is easy with us. But you could also choose to give up on the dream of becoming your own boss." (Too harsh? We can always adjust.)

- "Choosing to start now so you have a chance to work out of your home is a good choice. But you also have an option not to start now, and keep commuting in that rush-hour traffic you hate forever."
- "Choosing an extra income for our family is a choice, but we can also choose to get by on one paycheck too."
- "Choosing to work towards financial independence is a good choice, but some people choose not to." (Too direct?)

We get the idea.

But could we also use this with team members? Sure.

- "Choosing to learn new skills to build our business is a choice. But we can also choose to stay where we are."
- "Choosing to get a convention ticket now is a great idea. But we could also delay and hope the convention doesn't sell out and leave us without a ticket."
- "Choosing to talk to our friends and relatives first is a good choice. But we could also wait until later, and hope they don't feel slighted because we talked to others first."

How many choices should we give someone?

Two.

More choices create confusion. We know the old saying, "A confused mind always says 'No.'"

Two choices mean there will be an outcome one way or the other. And that is what we want. The "I need to think it over" objection will now go away.

Multiple choices? Bad idea. Brain science tells us that more choices create indecision. Let's keep our choices at only two.

Detach ourselves from the outcome.

Our obligation is to let prospects know they have options. We do our best to describe the options. To make this more clear, we can say this.

"I cannot make your decision for you. Sorry, you have to do it yourself."

No rejection. Just choices. And our prospects make their choices.

Prepare ourselves for the decision.

Some prospects desperately hang on to the "I need to think it over" excuse. They hope something happens in the future that will make their decisions for them. They don't want to be responsible for the personal decisions they make in their lives. How does that sound in real life?

"This is too hard. I am a professional victim. My father died broke, my grandfather died broke, and I want to die broke like them. I feel like jumping off a cliff. Would you please help and give me a push? I like it when people feel sorry for me."

Okay. Slightly enhanced, but we see the pattern. If someone insists on not making decisions, it is okay to let it go. Our business may not be for them. They will have to make many business decisions in the future with our business. Our business is not for everyone.

More objections in our future?

Of course.

Let's take a look at a few more common objections now.

"THIS IS TOO EXPENSIVE!"

If we have never heard this objection before, that means we never talked to anyone.

This is a common "go-to" objection that prospects use often. This objection could mean that they don't see value in our offer. Or, it could be a delay tactic because they feel scared to make a decision.

How common is this objection? Every networker gets it. And what is surprising is that few networkers learn how to handle it effectively. They don't plan. They hope something will come to their minds at the last moment. Not a good strategy.

Before we create a structure or template to handle this common objection, let's look at some fun ideas from others.

My friend, Tom Paredes, tells this story.

"I had one team member mail a product catalog with a price list. She did a follow-up call. Her prospects reply, 'All the products are too expensive.' Most people would have said, 'Oh okay, sorry.' But my team member said, 'Well, you know the prices I sent you were retail prices. Did you know that you can get them cheaper if you are a member?'

"And the prospect said, 'Ohhh!' Now, it opened the door for more conversation. Sometimes we have to ask more questions."

Jonathan Yap likes to make an instant comparison. He says, "This is the difference between a Bentley and a Toyota." For ladies, Jonathan would ask them to compare the difference between a Louis Vuitton and a cheap $10 bag from a garage sale. Then Jonathon would refocus the prospect on the quality of the products.

Dale Moreau has a great answer that helps prospects see value in our offer. This is from his book, *LinkedIn for Network Marketing: How to Unleash the Power of LinkedIn to Build Your Network Marketing Business.*

"You are right for saying our product is expensive. Our product is a treat or luxury. It is like spending money on golf, a day at the spa, buying stuff off Amazon, eating out with friends, or drinking at the bar."

In our book, *How to Build Network Marketing Leaders Volume One: Step-By-Step Creation of MLM Professionals*, we do a long, logical comparison that shows how people don't buy on price. Instead, people buy on convenience, quality, comfort, extra features, or prestige. Most people pay more for products when they can get this extra convenience, quality, comfort, extra features, or prestige.

Think about our lives. Does everyone buy the cheapest:

- Jewelry? That would mean only costume jewelry would sell.
- Car? Not everyone drives the cheapest model of car.
- Shoes? Haha. No chance. Check out shoe prices today.
- The cheapest mobile phone?

We get the picture.

But what is my favorite way to handle the "too expensive" objection?

The ten-second challenge.

Unfortunately, our prospects make quick and harsh judgments about us. When prospects make objections, they use our first few words to set their minds about us and what we have to offer. It isn't fair, but it is what happens.

This is why we must prepare for this common objection before we talk to prospects. We won't have time for a long, rambling answer. Let's take a look at what our answer must do.

1. Agree with our prospects.
2. Explain why we are more expensive.
3. Destroy the cheaper competition.
4. Satisfy our prospects so that no more discussion is needed.

Thankfully, this isn't hard. Here is the technique from our book, *Quick Start Guide for Network Marketing*.

• • •

When our prospects tell us that our product is too expensive, we will reply:

"Yes, it is expensive. The company wanted to make a cheaper version, but they knew it wouldn't work. And, they didn't want to rip you off."

This is an easy answer to memorize. And, we only took a couple of seconds.

Let's see what the words do.

"Yes, it is expensive." We agree with our prospects. Our prospects don't have to think of more facts or excuses to support their position. Now their minds are free. And when their minds are free, what will they do? Listen to us! This is good.

"The company wanted to make a cheaper version." Every company would love to make a cheaper version. If the final product only costs a few pennies, millions more could buy and afford it. But unfortunately, this is impossible. Stuff costs money to make.

"But, they knew it wouldn't work." Now our prospects think, "A cheaper version of this product would not work as well." To our prospects, our product now has more value. It needs to be this price to work effectively. When our prospects see competing products that are cheaper, what do we think our prospects will think? Yes, our prospects will think, "Yes, this is cheaper. But, I am sure they had to compromise and cut out a lot of value to get it at this price. It probably won't work for me."

"And they did not want to rip you off." We don't need to add this, but it is so much fun to say. Why? It makes us feel good about our company. It makes our prospects feel good about our company. And the next time our prospects see a cheaper version of our product, they will think, "If I buy this, it probably won't work as well. I will be ripped off."

• • •

This is an easy formula to follow for any product, service or even for the startup costs to join our opportunity.

The main point we want to remember is this. We only have a few seconds. Our words must be compact and direct. When we do this with confidence, our prospects feel good about associating with professionals like us.

Let's do one more related objection.

"I don't want to join your opportunity until I first use the products myself."

Pretty good objection.

Our prospects wish to judge the value of our business based on their personal experiences with our products or services.

Bad logic.

For example, imagine at the end of our presentation, our prospect gives us the "I don't want to join your opportunity until I first use the products myself" objection.

What if some of our products won't work for the prospect? What if some products are gender-specific, or age-specific? Does that mean we have a bad opportunity for our prospects?

No.

If our prospects are of average weight and we market weight-loss products, chances are our prospects will be disappointed with the results of our weight-loss products.

Does that mean our weight-loss products wouldn't be of great service to our prospects' potential customers? Our prospects could build a tremendous business if they had access to lots of fat people (vertically-challenged, under-tall, person-of-weight, calorie-handicapped, etc. for those wishing to be politically correct).

The real questions our prospects should ask?

"Is there a market for these products?" (Yes. There are plenty of overweight people.)

"Will people buy these products?" (Yes. People want to fix their problems.)

To answer this objection we could say, "Personal experience with our products is nice, but the big picture is if other people will use our products. Over 10,000 people have said 'Yes' already. We just have to let people know."

Two easy objections from skeptical prospects.

"So how much money have you made so far?"

If we are new or unsuccessful, we fear this question. Amateurs create evasive answers that create even more skepticism in prospects, such as:

"Oh, you wouldn't believe."

"It is top secret. If I told you, I would have to kill you."

Cheesy. So let's do better.

The classic and most accurate answer is:

"I don't know. I haven't finished collecting it all yet."

So true. We don't know how much or how long we will be collecting from someone we sold to or sponsored in our first month. And even if we didn't get customers or team members our first month, we still don't know if the seeds we planted then will pay off later.

This answer is good as it introduces the residual income concept to prospects.

But what if our prospects don't find this answer satisfying? Or what if our career is a disaster to date? Then, let's continue to be truthful. Here is what we could say:

"So far? Nothing. This is a real business. Like all business start-ups, it will take several months for me to make a good profit. And with my first profits, I am going to take a one-week cruise and celebrate. I only wanted to know if you would like to join me now, so we could take a cruise together. Or, if you would rather give me your home address, I can send you a picture postcard from my cruise."

This answer gives a more realistic future to our skeptical prospects. They don't feel misdirected. The answer is satisfying. And we don't have to explain our initial incompetency. Yes, most of us had less than awesome starts in our network marketing businesses.

"What is the catch?"

A short answer to this skeptic's question?

"The 'catch' is that this isn't a no-effort, get-rich-quick scheme or a lottery. We are building a business that can pay us monthly. This is a business we can be proud of."

Done.

PREVENTION.

Outside my window, my local squirrels play. Because I live in a jungle setting, my squirrels have a limited lifespan. Bad things happen. It isn't like the animal life in Disney movies.

Every month or so, there is a rotation of new squirrels. While I don't have a long-term relationship with my rotating squirrel population, they are more than happy to accept food from me, the overweight stranger. Their hunger and desire for fresh food help them overcome their fear of me.

Must we build relationships before prospecting strangers?

No.

Of course, talking to a friend would be easier. We are then starting with some trust and rapport. But ...

When cold prospects are hungry, they will make decisions on what we offer, even if we don't have a relationship with them.

Hungry prospects, with a problem, looking for change ... are the best. They take steps to solve their problems now. Their objections feel small compared to their desire to solve their problem. The bigger the problem our prospects want to solve, the less important their objections become.

So yes, having a relationship makes sponsoring easier. But we can still build and move forward, even if we don't have a relationship yet. The key is to focus on the big problem our prospects want to solve.

I prevent squirrel objections by bringing nuts with me when I walk outside. Here is how we can have a better start with our prospects.

Worried about objections at the end of our presentations?

What is the easiest way to avoid the drama at the end of our presentations? To sort out the commitment before our presentations start. Here is an example. Instead of introducing a big price at closing, we can say this before our presentations start:

"Before I share this business, one thing bothers me. Most people love our business, but some can't afford the $500 start-up cost. Do you think this would be a problem for you?"

If our prospects say that it isn't a problem, the presentation will be easy. If our prospects say it might be a problem, now is a good time to know. We can adjust our presentation.

When prospects know the cost before we start, they can focus on our presentation. They won't have a nagging interruption in the back of their minds saying, "I wonder when this salesman is going to spring the price on me? How much does this cost?" This reduces the pressure our prospects feel.

Another question to prevent objections?

"Are you ready for a change?"

That's it. Then allow our prospects to tell us if they are ready for a change in their lives ... or not.

If they want a change, then the rest of our presentation is easy. They make a "yes" decision before we start.

"There are two types of people in the world."

We can start by saying, "There are two types of people in the world. Those who look for reasons why, and those that look for reasons why not."

This opening puts our prospects in an "open-minded" attitude. No one wants to feel they are closed-minded. Now they will look for reasons why this opportunity can work for them, instead of looking for reasons not to join.

When we use this phrase to start a presentation, we won't need to use pressure or harsh closing techniques. When our prospects are open-minded, no manipulation is needed. They can judge for themselves if this opportunity fits their needs or not.

"What will happen if you don't join our business?"

This is a great question to ask after we find out our prospects' problems, and before we start our presentation. This question helps in two areas:

#1. It lets our prospects know this is a "Yes" or "No" moment in their lives. They either take our upcoming solution to their problems, or make a decision not to take our solution, and keep their lives the same.

#2. It reminds our prospects their current pain will continue if they don't make a decision to fix it. The more our prospects describe what "staying where they are" would feel like, the more motivation they create for change.

Variations on this prevention question could be:

- "Do you think the weight will go away and normalize on its own?"
- "What do you think your chances are for a big 25% salary increase this year?"
- "Do you see yourself as a jobholder, working for someone else, all your life?"
- "Do you think a judge will grant us mercy in court, just because we can't afford a lawyer?"
- "Does the city have any plans to build more and faster roads to your job? Do you think traffic will get better?"
- "How long do you think our children can wait until we finally get to spend more time with them?"

When the reasons to fix their problems are huge, our prospects feel that their objections are small.

"I don't have time."

We hate negative talkers. Most people spend three hours a week complaining about their jobs and stupid bosses. Another hour per week is spent discussing bad decisions from politicians. Then there is the time to discuss the in-laws. Here is a way we can put those wasted hours to work for us.

Most prospects smile and realize that they could use a few minutes of their non-productive time to build a networking business. We don't ask prospects to give up this chatter time with their friends. We only ask them to change the subject of their chatter for a few minutes.

Everyone has 24 hours in a day. It's how we choose to use those 24 hours that counts. We can't give prospects more time, but we can give them an option of what they do with some of their time.

The ultimate skeptics.

Green personalities, such as engineers and accountants, are careful to avoid mistakes when making decisions. They have non-verbalized fears and objections that keep them from seeing our benefits. If we sold discounted electricity, here is an example.

Our skeptical prospects think:

- What if the new electricity supplier goes out of business? Will I be cut off? No lights or power?
- What if the service is substandard?
- What if the fine print of this new contract allows them to supersize my bill?
- Who will fix my electricity after a storm?

To eliminate these fears before we start, we could preempt their objections by saying:

"Everyone gets the same electricity on our national grid. Nothing will change. Same electricity. Same service. Same repairmen. The only thing that will change is that we will send you a slightly lower bill. That is why there is no need for us to continue over-paying our current bill. Would you like to see what your new bill would look like with your savings?"

Could we use this same tactic for nutrition, skincare, travel, legal, insurance or even our business opportunity? Yes.

The secret is to let our prospects know that "Nothing will change." This makes the decision feel safer. An opportunity example?

"Relax. Starting a part-time business won't affect your current job or paycheck. The only thing that will change is that you will have more money every month. Would that make things easier for you?"

Prospects love safety and security.

WHO GIVES US OBJECTIONS?

The good news is that objections come from interested prospects. If they had no interest, we wouldn't be this far into the conversation. They wouldn't waste their time talking to us.

Consider this.

1. We offer something great to our prospects.
2. Our prospects want it but are afraid to take the first step.

If we take this viewpoint, we won't look at objections as live/die or a win/lose conversation. Instead, we will reassure our prospects that we will help them be safe as they take their first step.

So instead of hiding from objections, we should be thankful. Our prospect is saying, "I am looking for a solution to my problem, so I can move forward. Can you help me?"

The good news about objections? Our prospects know exactly what is bothering them and holding them back. And better yet, they tell us!

Now we can concentrate on helping them move forward as a customer or as a new team member.

Are some objections legitimate?

Of course. Here are a few reasons our prospects won't want what we offer.

- Our prospects don't need what we offer.
- Our prospects fear change.
- Our prospects fear the unknown future.
- Our prospects don't understand.
- Our prospects reacted to us when we said the wrong words.
- Our prospects don't trust us.
- Our prospects don't want to be sold.
- Our prospects hold different beliefs and programs contrary to our message.

Yes, there are many reasons some prospects won't buy or join. It is okay.

There are 7.5 billion people who haven't joined network marketing yet. Plenty to choose from. And the good news? Our success doesn't depend on any particular prospect. If what we offer isn't a good fit, no problem. There are so many others to talk to.

"NOT INTERESTED."

Why is this objection so common? Because people have good manners. They are polite. They don't want to tell us "No!" to our faces. Why?

They could be relatives or friends. They want to let us down gently. Maybe they recently had a bad experience with a pushy salesman. Or they want to avoid conflict.

"I am not interested" can be said in so many ways. For example:

"I need time to think about this."

"Can I get back to you later?"

"Got a sample for me to look at first?"

"Let's talk about this later."

"The products are too expensive for me right now."

"Do you have a business card?"

"Got a brochure?"

"I need to check with my spouse first."

"I don't have time to check it out now. Possibly later."

"What is the website so I can look at it later?"

These are ways our prospects tell us, "No, I am not interested." They want us to go away or change the subject.

How can we answer the "not interested" objection?

If we refuse to take the hint, and want to give it our best shot, here are some answers from salesmen on how they handle this objection.

- "You don't have to be interested. Just find people who are interested, and you can still earn good money."

- "You are right. You shouldn't be interested in our business. However, you might be interested in getting an extra check from our business. That would help pay for Heather's school."

- "The last two people I talked to said exactly that. When they found out they could work out of their homes instead of commuting, they wanted to know more. Would you like to know what they found out?"

- "Of course. It is hard to be interested because I failed to tell you how much money you can earn. Is it okay if I give you the evidence? Then, it is up to you."

- "I know you are too busy to be interested now. I can help you have more time. Could we talk about it during lunch one day, so it wouldn't take away any of your precious time?"

Sounds too salesy?

Of course it depends on the situation and who we talk to.

Then what would be a better solution?

Prevention.

Maybe we should be more interesting. This could be a hint.

How will we be more interesting?

First, listen better. Try to find the problem our prospects want to solve. When we talk about our prospects' problems, they feel we are the most interesting people in the world.

Second, could we describe our solution better? There is a difference when we use positive phrases such as:

- "We message people anyway."
- "This fits in with our normal conversations every day."
- "Most people have fun passing on these options."
- "This can open up a whole new world for us."

These phrases feel more positive than saying, "Be brave. Just talk to everyone."

MAKE IT THEIR PROBLEM.

This technique we can use as prevention, and also as an immediate reply to our prospects' objections. Here are the magic words:

"What will happen if you don't <solve this problem>?"

Here is how this will sound in real life.

Our prospects complain, "I don't have enough money every month. But I don't want to spend my Saturdays working to build a part-time business."

We can reply, "I understand. But what will happen if you don't get the extra money you need every month?"

Now our prospects will create a movie inside of their heads of their money problems persisting. They may think:

"If I don't build an extra income, I will have to work overtime forever. I won't see my kids, I will have no free time, and I hate this routine. I don't want to work this hard until I die."

Now our prospects feel more open-minded about our option. Why? Because they realize they don't have any other options! Let's try a few more of these.

Prospects: "This sounds too hard."

Us: "Yes, it isn't easy when we first start. But what will happen if you don't build a better income? Will you still hate the morning alarm you complain about?"

Prospects: "I don't know if I want to risk this. I may not be successful."

Us: "Yes, that is always a possibility. But what will happen if we never try? That means we will continue to be frustrated with our situation."

Prospects: "I don't want to sell to my family and friends."

Us: "Totally understand. I don't want to either. But what will happen if we don't let them know how this could help them lose weight? If they find out later that we kept this secret from them, they could be upset."

Want more objection-destroying phrases we can say to get our prospects to help them to overcome their reluctance?

1. "What will happen if we can't keep our skin from wrinkling as we get older?"
2. "What will happen if we can't lose our weight?"
3. "What will happen if we have to continue commuting every day for life?"
4. "What will happen if we can't save enough money for their college educations?"
5. "What will happen if we continue working at this salary?"

What if we want a little variety in this question?

"How else can we lower our utilities instantly?"

"How else can we be our own boss without making a big investment?"

"How else are we going to be able to fire our boss?"

"How else are we going to make our bodies younger?"

"How else can we stop our aging?"

"How else are we going to be able to pay this new mortgage rate increase?"

"How else will we ever catch up and pay off our credit cards?"

Again, all we are doing is helping our prospects understand their choices. They can take advantage of our offer, or continue living their lives the same, keeping their frustrations and problems.

MUST WE ANSWER
EVERY OBJECTION?

Four rejections in a row. I couldn't believe it.

It was a late, rainy Sunday evening. Art Jonak and I were leaving a night market in Thailand.

I asked to hire the first taxi driver in the line to take us to our next stop. "No." That was a short reply. The second taxi driver at least paused before announcing, "No."

I was getting soaked in the rain.

Taxi driver #3 and taxi driver #4 didn't want to take us where we wanted to go either.

And now, the decision.

Choice #1: Should I try to convince the first four taxi drivers to change their minds, handle their objections, and schedule a follow-up? Or,

Choice #2: Should I ask taxi driver #5 for a ride?

The rainwater was running down the back of my pants, so I opted for choice #2. I asked taxi driver #5 if he would take us to where we wanted to go.

Turned out taxi driver #5 was more than happy to take Art Jonak and a soaked Big Al to where we wanted to go. He didn't even mind the damp spot I left on the back seat covers.

When we are in a hurry, and getting rained on, rejection doesn't seem to bother us much. We just get on with doing what we have to do to get the job done.

If we hate rejection, one way of dealing with our feelings is to be in a hurry. Have more and better prospects to talk to. Then, we don't have time to feel bad for ourselves.

TREATING OBJECTIONS AS QUESTIONS, NOT CHALLENGES.

Instead of reacting to our prospects' objections, let's reframe their objections as a question or as a challenge.

Careful here. We don't want to appear to be a manipulative salesman using verbal jujitsu. We want to simply look at the objection from a more positive viewpoint. Remember, our prospects react to what we do.

Focusing on the objection as a challenge.

If our prospects bring up an objection, we can start with two different viewpoints.

#1. Our prospects don't want to buy. Or,

#2. Our prospects want what we offer, but they see something standing in their way. They want our help to remove that obstacle.

The second viewpoint has less stress and better reactions from our prospects. Here is a short, abrupt example of turning an objection into a challenge.

Prospect: "It is too expensive."

Us: "So our objective is to make this affordable for you."

Abrupt. We have the idea, but we need friendlier words. How about responding like this?

Prospect: "It is too expensive."

Us: "I understand. This can help you so much, but it doesn't fit your current budget. Should we look at ways to make this more affordable for you? So that you can get what you want?"

We change the conversation from "It is too expensive" to "How can I afford this?" Now we can work on this new objection, hand-in-hand, with our prospects.

As a bonus, this type of reply carries the assumption that our prospects want what we offer. Now we are not fighting the decision to buy or not. Instead, we are taking on the challenge of how to make it affordable.

More examples of this technique?

Prospects: "No way I could take on another job or part-time business."

Us: "Yes, you are pressed for time. No way could you fit in another 10 hours a week in your packed schedule. Should we look at ways of how to work this business in just two concentrated hours every week? Then you can get that extra money you need."

If our prospects say "No" to our offer of fitting our business into their schedule, what does that tell us? We now know that "time" is not the problem. There must be another hidden objection they are not telling us.

More examples.

Prospects: "I dieted all my life. Spent a fortune. Nothing works for me. I don't want to waste money on this."

Us: "Wow. That must feel bad. Sorry to hear about all the frustrations. I would hate that experience too! Should we look at a way to lose weight one time, and keep it off forever? Would that make things feel better?"

Prospects: "I don't want to change my service. It's too much hassle to save only a few dollars."

Us: "Yeah, I agree. No one wants to spend an hour on hold with the cell phone provider getting a run-around, and then only saving $6 a month from that hassle. Our time is worth more than that. You know, $6 a month is more than $70 each year in overcharges. Should we look at a way to do this in less than 10 minutes? So can we stop their overcharging?"

Prospects: "I am not interested. I can't set an appointment."

Us: "Yes, that is what most people say before we meet. But would you like to know why they change their mind?"

Prospects: "I am not a people person. I am shy. I won't feel comfortable talking to people."

Us: "So true. I know how you feel. Many of us feel the same way. Would you like to know what we do so that we never feel bad talking to and helping people?"

Turning objections into questions means less tension. This can give us the opportunity to have a better conversation with our prospects.

PART TWO.

Answering objections. A great skill to have.

> Q. What would be an even better skill than answering objections?
>
> A. Preventing objections.

In the second part of this book, let's upgrade our objections skills.

Prevention.

This is what leaders do. They learn how to prevent objections from happening.

Let's go!

"WHAT IS BETTER THAN SCAMMY SCARCITY AND URGENCY TACTICS?"

Scarcity and urgency manipulations feel artificial. Prospects don't like those tactics. We don't either. We cringe when we resort to saying, "We only have a few of these left. Act now. I can only offer you this sales price tonight."

If scarcity, urgency, and other artificial manipulations interest you, this isn't the book for you. Instead, let's take a better road to dealing with tough objections.

We can fight objections, or we can change the conversation.

Change the conversation? There is an old saying:

"When we have a vision, nothing gets in our way.

"And when we don't have a vision, everything gets in our way."

And what does that mean for objections?

Everything!

When we give our prospects a vision of a successful future, present obstacles and objections fade away. Excuses, barriers, and problems seem small when compared to a brilliant vision for the future.

When we give our prospects a great vision, we can ignore their trivial objections and obstacles. Yes, a great way to handle many objections is to ignore the objections. Then, focus on a brilliant outcome from taking advantage of what we offer.

Imagine that we visit a city with the world's greatest pizza. But, it will take us 45 minutes to get to this special pizzeria. Maybe we will have to wait in line. And it won't be cheap. However, we can't wait to taste that delicious pizza everyone raves about.

Did we overcome or fix any of our objections and obstacles? No. Our vision of biting into that delicious pizza makes us ignore the obstacles. We are going for pizza!

Vision rocks.

But what is an easy way to create this vision for our prospects? Here is the answer. And it is brilliant!

Word pictures.

Is this the most powerful network marketing skill ever? Possibly. With the skill of crafting exciting word pictures inside of our prospects' minds comes ... confidence. And these word pictures are so much fun to do.

How did I learn the power of word pictures?

Almost 50 years ago, at the beginning of my career, I gave one of my best presentations. The result? My prospect didn't join! Shocking I know, but it happens. He said that network marketing wasn't for him.

Three days later I ran across the same prospect, and he had joined another opportunity! Not just any opportunity – he had joined a Ponzi, pyramid, seventeenth-generation, photocopied chain letter straight from prison. A real piece of garbage!

Now if that were to happen to you, what would cross your mind?

I decided to take personal responsibility for my results. Instead of blaming the prospect, I decided to accept that my results were caused by … me.

So here is the question that crossed my mind:

"What did his sponsor say to him that I didn't?"

Good question. I decided to find out.

I always wanted to do this – it's straight out of a 'B' movie – so I said to my former hot prospect:

"Take me to your leader!"

We went to see his new leader and I told his leader:

"I'm the famous Big Al, I wrote these books, I've got this big group. I bet you spent a lot of time, maybe even the entire three days, trying to get this young man to join your business."

His sponsor calmly replied, "It took me about 90 seconds."

I felt about one inch tall. My inflated opinion of myself … destroyed.

His new leader continued, "Big Al, you have a problem. Your problem is you speak in words."

Right away I thought, "Well, what are the options here?"

His new leader then dropped the bombshell. He said, "People don't think in words, they think in pictures."

This is the breakthrough that helped me understand how things work in the "real world."

"Pink Elephant."

What happens if someone yells out these words?

"Pink Elephant!"

Huh? Pink Elephant? What goes on in our minds? If they unscrewed the top of our heads, looked inside, what would they see? A giant letter "P" ... and then the letter "I" ... and then ... no! That isn't how it works.

We don't think in letters or in words. We think in pictures.

The words "Pink Elephant" instantly create a picture of a soft, kind, smiling elephant in pink. Our minds take words and turn those words into vivid pictures in our minds. This phenomenon is key. This is the shortcut professionals always dreamed of.

How to transfer information fast.

What would happen if everybody we talked to knew exactly what we knew? In other words, if all the information in our brain was in their brain – they would make the same decision that we did.

The problem is, our prospects are not going to sit for three days while we tell them all of our experiences–so they can see exactly what we see.

But a picture is worth a thousand words!

Now, I never tested this claim. It could be 973 words or something—but a picture transfers information a thousand times faster from our brain to our prospects' brains. By using pictures, our prospects can see what we see. Communication means that if they see what we see, they are going to join.

Word pictures are fun because prospects see in their minds what we see in our minds. They see our vision. They see our excitement.

Are word pictures complicated, long, and difficult to do?

Word pictures can take a few seconds or a few minutes. For an example of a very short word picture, imagine this.

A young lady goes to the beach. Later, she tells her father that she saw this nice young man at the beach. Then she would give her father a one-word word picture and say:

"Wow!"

That word creates a picture in the father's mind. Maybe not the exact same picture that was in his daughter's mind, but she did instantly create a picture.

Children use word pictures.

Imagine we have a six-year-old daughter. She goes to school on the first day and all the kids in the class are wearing a special type of uniform, except for her. Her clothes are different.

Her classmates make fun of her. They tease her. Our daughter cries. During recess, her classmates don't play with her. They make her stand in the corner of the playground, facing traffic, insisting that she doesn't look at them.

The first day of school was very traumatic for our daughter.

On the way home from school, our six-year-old daughter plots, "Well, I can tell Mom and Dad that I need a uniform. But they don't see what I see. They won't feel what I feel. They won't buy me a new uniform. I will have to use a word picture on Mom and Dad, so they see and feel what I see and feel. Then they will buy me a uniform."

Our daughter arrives home and says:

"Mom, Dad, I was at school today and all the other kids had a special uniform except for me. They teased me. They made fun of me. I tried not to cry. I tried to be brave like you told me, but I started to cry and tears ran down my face.

"I felt embarrassed. I felt bad. But then at recess, they made me stand at the corner of the playground with my back to them facing traffic. They wouldn't even let me look at them. I had to stand there crying.

"And all day long none of my classmates would look at me or play with me. It was awful!"

While our daughter is giving this word picture, what are we doing? We are grabbing the credit card and heading to the store to get that uniform because we see what she sees.

As your daughter gets older, her word pictures get better and better. Soon, she gets everything she wants!

Kids are great at using word pictures. They have plenty of time to practice their word pictures while their parents are working.

I joined because of a word picture.

In 1972, my wife and I went to our first opportunity meeting. We answered an ad in the newspaper that said:

"Part-time business. Small investment."

We came to the Saturday morning business opportunity meeting and it was three hours long. There was a bunch of anti-government, Communist hippies, talking about strange things coming out of their colons, and a lot of cheering from the crowd of weird people.

At the end of this three-hour meeting, my wife and I looked at each other and said, "Let's get out of here. The armed guards are gone from the back door."

So we are sneaking out of the back of the room. Just then, the person who ran the ad recognized us because we were the only guests. He said, "Aren't you the people who answered the ad?"

We mumbled back, "Yes, but it looks like it is not for us. We are not interested and much too busy."

My sponsor looked at me and gave me a little 30-second word picture which was more powerful than the three-hour meeting. This word picture earned my sponsor a lot of money. Yes, a single word picture could earn us a fortune!

Would you like to hear the word picture my sponsor told me?

My sponsor said:

"Big Al, when you join our business here is what happens. Six months from now you walk into your boss' office. You sit down in the chair, you put your feet up on his desk and you leave little scuff marks with your heels.

"You put your hands behind your head and calmly tell the boss that you can't fit him into your schedule any longer. You have enjoyed working there, so if they have any problem after you leave they can call you any Tuesday morning at 11 o'clock at your normal consulting rate.

"Then you get up from the boss' office, walk out to the main office desk, pick up your personal belongings, wave good-bye to all your fellow workers who said it couldn't be done, hop into your brand-new bonus car, drive down to the bank drive-in teller window, deposit this month's bonus check, and say to the bank teller:

"'Oh, I don't know. Put this bonus check in savings or checking. It really doesn't matter. I get these checks every month.'

"And then you drive home and relax, having a nice glass of your favorite beverage."

That was his word picture. At the end of his word picture, I said: "So how do I join?"

I enrolled based on that 30-second word picture, not because of the three-hour opportunity meeting.

My sponsor was able to get me to see "what he saw" in the business. My sponsor created a vision in my mind because of that simple 30-second word picture.

Would you like to have a formula so you could create word pictures too?

Here is our formula. Simply say:

"When you join our business, here is what happens ..."

Then, take our listeners into the future and let them know exactly what is going to happen.

That's it! Pretty simple, wasn't it?

Want more examples?

Example #1.

This is an example of creating a word picture about receiving a bonus check in the mail for $100. Notice how this short word picture creates a story or a movie in our prospects' minds.

"When you join our business, here is what happens. Two months from now you walk out to your mailbox and you get your mail. Now there is some junk mail and magazines, but there is also a letter from your network marketing company.

"When you get inside the house, you rip open the envelope and you look inside. It is not a letter from your network marketing company. It is a check. It is a check for $100 which you didn't expect. So you say, 'Hey, maybe I should go shopping or take the family out to dinner.'"

Well, did that short word picture create a story or movie in our minds? Could we see ourselves ripping open the envelope?

Instead of telling our prospects they can earn $100, use this word picture instead. Our prospects will think about this word picture every time they go to the mailbox, and that will remind them of our opportunity.

Example #2.

We can help our prospects create a vision of what they could do with a part-time check. Telling them they can earn an extra $750 a month is not as exciting as showing our prospects what they could do with the extra $750 a month. Here is an example of a word picture that does that:

"When you join our business, here is what happens. You go to the local car dealership and you say to the salesman, 'Hey! This is the car I would like.'

"The car salesman says, 'Okay, with your trade-in, that is going to be a $750 a month car payment.'

"You reply, 'No problem. I have a part-time business that will cover the payments for me.'"

Both of these examples were very simple and short word pictures. Of course we can do longer, more elaborate word pictures.

The key is to help our prospects see themselves in the word pictures that we create. We do this by starting our word pictures with this phrase:

"When you join our business, here is what happens."

Use word pictures every chance we get.

Word pictures are easy. We have unconsciously used them before in our lives. Now that we recognize exactly how to use word pictures, we will use them much more often.

Word pictures are preemptive. They help prevent objections.

But word pictures are also effective after an objection.

We should make word pictures an addiction.

Can we use word pictures to sell our products or services?

Of course. Here are the formulas:

1. "When you use our product, here is what happens."
2. "When you use our service, here is what happens."

That wasn't hard. Want some examples?

Example #1.

If we sold a diet product, we could say:

"When you use our diet product, here is what happens. One week from now you wake up and while putting on your clothes you notice – hey! The pants are baggy! You have lost an inch or two off your waist and you didn't even have to diet!"

Our prospects can see themselves trying on their pants in the morning. We created a movie in their minds.

Example #2.

If we sold a skincare product, we would say:

"When you use our skin cleanser, here is what happens. After you rinse off our special cleanser, feel your face with your fingertips. It will feel so smooth, like satin or silk!"

In our prospects' minds, they will see themselves feeling their soft skin.

Example #3.

If we represent an opportunity that sells credit repair services, we could say:

"When you use our credit repair service, here is what happens. Three months from now, you re-check your credit bureau score, and now your score is no longer in the high-risk, high-rate zone. You feel good that your credit scores won't hold you back any longer."

Now that is powerful. Why?

Because if our prospects don't use our credit repair service, what will they think every time they needed a better credit score? They will think of us and our offer. Over and over again.

And finally, after more bad credit reports, it will be time for our prospects to take action with us. We will be in their minds already.

Example #4.

Our prospects object, "I don't want to change my electricity provider. I don't want to bother."

We could say, "I understand. But when we change our electricity provider to a lower cost, here is what happens. Starting immediately, with our very next bill, we save money. And we can accumulate these savings to pay for that family holiday we always dreamed of. And every time we get our electricity bill, we smile. We will know we are one step closer to that dream family experience everyone wants. Taking six minutes to change our provider online could mean a lifetime of memories for our family."

Keep our word pictures simple and listener-friendly.

Sometimes we try to sound important and super-intelligent. When we are new, we want to impress our prospects with our knowledge.

Bad idea.

Our job is to communicate clearly. We want our prospects to see exactly what we see in our business or products. If we are unclear, we will prompt objections. Prospects won't agree to something they don't understand.

Here is an example of a pompous "I am smart" presentation:

"Let me tell you about this unique amino acid found underneath a rock on a mossy hill in China, by a team of nuclear scientists who have movie stars as partners. Our Nobel Prize-winning scientists have patented a proprietary way of encapsulating this amino acid into a time-release formula that not only makes amputated body parts grow back, but it also creates world peace."

We don't like to be talked to this way, and our prospects won't like it any better.

So instead of this pompous drivel, let's throw out our technical data, our pretty brochures, and cancel all the three-hour opportunity meetings. Instead, we will do a better job of communicating with our prospects by using short word pictures.

Vision overcomes objections.

Remember, when the vision is big enough, nothing will get in our prospects' way. It is up to us to create this brilliant vision.

But what if our prospects insist on procrastinating? Maybe they have a reason they can't act now. Then, what do we do?

No problem. Here is our plan.

1. Create a vision for the future.
2. Set an automatic timer to remind our prospects of their vision.

We know that constant reminders work. When the time is right for our prospects, our constant reminders mean we will be front and center of their attention.

An example of how this would work in real life?

At the end of our presentation, our prospects object to moving forward. They say, "Oh no. The timing is all wrong in my life.

Plus I have to think everything over for days before I make final decisions."

Okay. If they choose the limitation that their decisions must be pondered for days, toilet breaks will be a problem. All kidding aside, imagine they insist that their current decision is "No" and that they will think about it in the future.

Prospects have other events in their lives. They won't think about us much unless we take action. So our first step? Agree.

We will say, "Relax. Think it over. Take all the time you want."

Our prospects feel relieved. No pressure from us. We agree with them. And how do they feel about us now? Great. So now will be a good time to ask them a favor.

"Tomorrow morning when your alarm wakes you up to go to work, can you ask yourself this little question?"

Prospects reply, "Sure."

We continue. "Ask yourself if you really want to get out of bed to fight traffic to that job you hate, or if it would be better if you could be your own boss, and work out of your home. Could you do that for me?"

Prospects smile, "Of course. I can do that."

What happened? What did we do?

1. Create a vision for the future.
2. Set an automatic timer to remind our prospects of their vision.

What happens the next morning?

Our prospects wake up, rub their eyes, feel unrested, and think:

"Ugh! Do I really want to be getting up at 7 a.m. in the morning, leaving my family, and fighting traffic to that stupid job? Maybe I should rethink that part-time business opportunity from last night."

Our plan succeeded. Our prospects remember the vision we gave them, and the alarm clock is the automatic reminder to remember us.

But here is the magic. What will happen the next morning? The same thoughts will go through our prospects' minds.

And the next morning . . .

And the next morning . . .

Our prospects get a daily morning reminder of our business opportunity. And when the timing is right (like a bad day at work, or a big traffic jam), we will be at the forefront of their minds. Our prospects will call us when the time is right for them to take action.

Instead of fighting their objection to delay, we will use vivid word pictures to help our prospects overcome their personal objections.

"Relax, think it over. Take all the time you want."

Great words to relax our prospects, and then introduce them to a happy vision for their futures. Prospects love it.

Need more examples? Let's go.

Skincare.

Our prospects hesitate. They tell us, "I bought an expensive moisturizer at the department store. Hasn't worked as the sales rep promised, but I still have three months' supply. Too expensive to throw out. Let me wait until I use it up, and then I will consider if I should buy your moisturizer."

We reply, "Relax, think it over. Take all the time you want. I understand. I felt the same way about my old moisturizer creams that I used. Every night when I went to sleep, when my head touched my pillow, I kept saying to myself, 'Do I want to continue to listen to my skin wrinkle every night while I sleep? Or do I want to start using the Wonderful Night Cream now?'"

1. Create a vision for the future.
2. Set an automatic timer to remind our prospects of their vision.

Well, guess what our prospect will think every evening when their heads touch their pillows? We might even be in their dreams.

Do we sell diet breakfast products?

Our prospects object. "I can't diet. I get hungry between snacks. I can't sleep on an empty stomach. Nothing works for me. I am big-boned. My metabolism is too slow. I enjoy being a professional victim!"

Ouch.

What are we going to do? Call our prospects every week and ask, "Hey, are you still fat?"

I don't think so. Instead …

We agree. We say, "Relax, think it over. Take all the time you want. By the way, could you do me a favor?"

Our chubby prospects relax, smile and say, "Sure. What is the favor?"

"Tomorrow morning, when you eat your breakfast, just before you put the first forkful in your mouth, could you ask yourself this question? 'Is this breakfast making me thinner and looking good? Or is this breakfast making me fat?' That's all. Could you do that for me?"

Guess what our prospects will think tomorrow morning, and every morning thereafter?

Done.

Electricity or phone plan savings.

Our prospects complain, "Oh, it is too much bother to change. I am okay with what I have. My family has never changed. It won't be worth my time to go through the hassle of changing."

And our reply?

"Relax, think it over. Take all the time you want. By the way, could you do me a favor?"

Our prospects breathe a sigh of relief and say, "Of course."

We continue. "You love taking your family out to eat at least once a month. That is great. But when it comes time to pay the dinner bill, could you ask yourself this question? 'Do I really want to be paying this dinner bill out of my pocket? Or maybe I should have switched my electricity and phone plans, and let those savings pay this bill, so we could eat for free.'"

And every month we will remind our prospects that our offer is waiting for them.

1. Create a vision for the future.
2. Set an automatic timer to remind our prospects of their vision.

So when all else fails, and our prospects continue to object, word pictures will be our next step. This is a great way to overcome even the toughest objections.

But want to take this vision to the next level?

VISION ON STEROIDS.

How can we create a bigger, more vivid vision in our prospects' minds? Let's learn how.

First, let's understand how things go into our minds. The only way we get things into our minds is by using our five senses.

What are the five senses?

Sight, hearing, smell, taste, and touch. (If you have more psychic powers, Vulcan mind control methods, etc., please feel free to use them too.)

The more of these five senses we put into our word picture vision, the more prospects will see themselves in that vision – and the more they will want their vision.

Want an example of a word picture that uses all five senses? Here is a story from our book, *How to Prospect, Sell and Build Your Network Marketing Business with Stories.*

• • •

How to Protect Yourself from a Machete-Wielding Neighbor.

Imagine that you have been a part-time network marketer for the past six months. You've saved every word-of-mouth advertising bonus check and now have enough money to take that dream vacation to Tahiti.

Your regular job paid your monthly expenses, so you were able to save all of those extra monthly bonus checks.

You go to your local airport, and as you enter the Air Tahiti jumbo jet, you think,

"It was a great decision to do a little network marketing on the side. If my business continues to improve, I'll be taking one of these nice vacations every three months! Thank goodness my sponsor told me about this network marketing opportunity."

When you arrive in Tahiti, you're taken to a glamorous beach. Gentle ocean waves help you relax in your hammock while the resort's staff delivers your favorite tropical beverage. The music is soothing. The wind is refreshing. And you can smell the barbecue teriyaki chicken on the grill just a few feet away.

Aaaahh! It doesn't get any better than this.

But wait!

You spot a small dot on the horizon, and it appears to be moving. Yes, it's definitely moving. The dot continues to grow. It's moving towards you.

After watching the dot grow larger and larger, you realize that the dot is actually a person. And, this person is dragging an old blanket behind him.

Soon that person walks right up to your hammock, spreads his old blanket on the sand, and plops down to catch some sun. You look down at the person on the blanket and suddenly realize that this person is your ...

Next door neighbor!

What a surprise! What a coincidence! You turn to your next-door neighbor and say,

"Hi."

Your surprised neighbor stutters:

"Uh, uh, uh, it's you. I can't believe this! Here we are, thousands of miles away from home and it's you right here next to me! This is incredible!"

You answer,

"I'm quite surprised too. How come you're here enjoying a nice holiday?"

Your next-door neighbor's face droops. His brow wrinkles and he sadly mumbles,

"Well, you know I live a miserable life. I have to keep three jobs going just to pay the rent for our family. I'm in debt up to my ears. My car loan is overdue. There is no chance to advance in my job. I don't have a penny to my name. I'm doomed!

"So I thought I might as well take a three-day holiday once in my miserable life, in order to have that single pleasant memory before I die. And to get here, I took out another loan, I maxed out all five of my credit cards, I stole the money in my kids' college savings account, and I even broke into their piggy banks, just to scrape together enough money for this ticket.

"And what about you? How come you're here?"

Now comes the moment of truth.

You say,

"I got started in my own part-time networking business about six months ago. It's really great. I get paid for just letting people know about it. So, I saved up the last few bonus checks, and here I am. This part-time business is so good, I'm thinking about taking another week's holiday here in three months. I tell you, this business is more than great! It's awesome. In fact, it's so wonderful that I ... uh, uh ... uh, I forgot to tell you about this, didn't I?"

Your neighbor's face turns red. Slowly he gets up from his blanket and walks to the ice carving by the teriyaki chicken grill. He grabs the razor-sharp machete and slowly starts walking towards you. As he draws back his arm ..."

Whoops. Better stop here before it gets ugly.

• • •

Could we see our neighbor with that machete?

Of course. Let's take a look at all the senses used in this word picture story.

1. Did we use the sense of sight? Yes, we saw the jumbo jet, the dot on the horizon, and we saw our neighbor coming with the machete.
2. Did we use smell? Yes, we smelled the teriyaki chicken.
3. Did we use taste? Yes, we tasted our favorite tropical beverage and the teriyaki chicken.
4. Did we use touch? We felt the comfortable first-class seat, and the warm tropical breeze.
5. Did we use hearing? Yes, the tropical music and the roar of the jet engines.

In this word picture story, we used all five senses. This made the story vivid in our minds.

Will this word picture story be enough to overcome our prospects' objections? Maybe. But the good news is that our story will create a vision and memory inside of our prospects' minds. They won't forget us and our offer.

Want another example of creating a vivid vision?

Our prospects hesitate. They want to wait until the time is right, conditions are perfect, and there will be no obstacles and challenges. Then they will start our business. Right. That will never happen. Possibly the wife wants to start a better future, but the husband doesn't want to put in the extra time. Because we were good listeners, we discovered her husband's love of fast cars. That will be the vision we will place in his mind. We will say this.

• • •

Let's say you saved all your bonus checks because you want to buy that dream car, a Ferrari. That morning you walk down to the dealership and you look inside the window and you see your dream car, a beautiful shiny Ferrari.

What color is that Ferrari?

If you are like most people, you pictured that Ferrari in your mind, and it is the color red. If you pictured a different color than red, well, it may be a sign of deep psychological problems ... just kidding.

You walk up to that Ferrari and you look at your reflection, you say "Wow! I deserve this."

No salesmen are around so you think, "Well, maybe I will sit in that car and see what it is like."

You slip into the Ferrari, adjust your seat, and smell that new car smell. You grip that steering wheel and you feel the leather seats and you say "Wow! What a car!"

You look around. Still no salesman in sight. You think, "I wonder what the sound system sounds like?" So you turn on the sound system and all ten speakers blare out your favorite song. Wow! It doesn't get any better than this!

Still no salesman. You think, "I wonder what the engine sounds like?" You gently turn the key – vroom, vroom – and even though you are in the showroom, the engine is so quiet that nobody notices. What a smooth-running, quiet engine! It sounds powerful!

Again, you look around – still no salesman. You grab the shifter and ease it into first gear, just to feel what the power would be like, and when you do that ...

Kaboom!

You fly right through the picture window, right out of the showroom! And as you turn the corner out of the parking lot at 90 miles an hour, you adjust your rearview mirror and you see the State Police f-a-d-i-n-g into the background.

• • •

The husband smiles. He will never get that vision out of his mind. Every time he sits in his 8-year-old Toyota, he reminds himself of what our business can do for him. Yes, there will be objections and obstacles, but this vision makes the sacrifices feel worthwhile.

What about us. Did we see the State Police, f-a-d-i-n-g into the background? Yes. This vision used several senses.

We used sight, hearing, smell, and touch. But we didn't use taste, did we?

We don't have to force all of the senses into every vision we create. Sometimes it won't make sense. We could force taste into this word picture and talk about the acrid taste as our prospect bit into that leather steering wheel, but that wouldn't make sense, would it?

Just use the senses that make sense.

Creating a powerful vision is easy if we remember this technique. Tell a word picture story that creates a movie inside our prospects' minds.

HOW DO WE FEEL ABOUT OBJECTIONS NOW?

When we have better ways to deal with our prospects' objections, our fears melt away. Objections are no longer that creepy, scary monster hiding beneath our beds. We can manage objections with better skills.

Are there more objections? Of course.

But we don't have to memorize an answer for every possible objection. Instead, once we learn the basics, we can create our own solutions when needed.

The basics?

First, we must agree. Nothing happens with closed-minded prospects.

And then, let's re-interpret our prospects' intentions. Objections can be their way of removing uncertainty in their decisions. Let's help them.

And finally, we can graduate to making word picture visions that are so vivid, our prospects will ignore the inconveniences to get those visions into their lives.

Have fun! And never fear objections again.

THANK YOU.

Thank you for purchasing and reading this book. We hope you found some ideas that will work for you.

Before you go, would it be okay if we asked a small favor? Would you take just one minute and leave a sentence or two reviewing this book online? Your review can help others choose what they will read next. It would be greatly appreciated by many fellow readers.

MORE BOOKS FROM BIG AL BOOKS

See them all at BigAlBooks.com

Mindset Series

Secrets to Mastering Your Mindset
Take Control of Your Network Marketing Career

Breaking the Brain Code
Easy Lessons for Your Network Marketing Career

How to Get Motivated in 60 Seconds
The Secrets to Instant Action

Prospecting and Recruiting Series

Hooks! The Invisible Sales Superpower
Create Network Marketing Prospects Who Want to Know More

How to Get Appointments Without Rejection
Fill Our Calendars with Network Marketing Prospects

Create Influence
10 Ways to Impress and Guide Others

How to Meet New People Guidebook
Overcome Fear and Connect Now

How to Get Your Prospect's Attention and Keep It!
Magic Phrases for Network Marketing

10 Shortcuts Into Our Prospects' Minds
Get Network Marketing Decisions Fast!

How To Prospect, Sell And Build Your Network Marketing Business With Stories

26 Instant Marketing Ideas To Build Your Network Marketing Business

51 Ways and Places to Sponsor New Distributors
Discover Hot Prospects For Your Network Marketing Business

First Sentences for Network Marketing
How To Quickly Get Prospects On Your Side

Big Al's MLM Sponsoring Magic
How To Build A Network Marketing Team Quickly

Start SuperNetworking!
5 Simple Steps to Creating Your Own Personal Networking Group

Getting Started Series

How to Build Your Network Marketing Business in 15 Minutes a Day

3 Easy Habits For Network Marketing
Automate Your MLM Success

Quick Start Guide for Network Marketing
Get Started FAST, Rejection-FREE!

Four Core Skills Series

How To Get Instant Trust, Belief, Influence and Rapport!
13 Ways To Create Open Minds By Talking To The Subconscious Mind

Ice Breakers!
How To Get Any Prospect To Beg You For A Presentation

Pre-Closing for Network Marketing
"Yes" Decisions Before The Presentation

The Two-Minute Story for Network Marketing
Create the Big-Picture Story That Sticks!

Personality Training Series (The Colors)

The Four Color Personalities for MLM
The Secret Language for Network Marketing

Mini-Scripts for the Four Color Personalities
How to Talk to our Network Marketing Prospects

Why Are My Goals Not Working?
Color Personalities for Network Marketing Success

How To Get Kids To Say Yes!
Using the Secret Four Color Languages to Get Kids to Listen

Presentation and Closing Series

Closing for Network Marketing
Getting Prospects Across The Finish Line

The One-Minute Presentation
Explain Your Network Marketing Business Like A Pro

How to Follow Up With Your Network Marketing Prospects
Turn Not Now Into Right Now!

Retail Sales for Network Marketers
How to Get New Customers for Your MLM Business

Leadership Series

The Complete Three-Book Network Marketing Leadership Series
Series includes: How To Build Network Marketing Leaders Volume
One, How To Build Network Marketing Leaders Volume Two, and
Motivation. Action. Results.

How To Build Network Marketing Leaders
Volume One: Step-By-Step Creation Of MLM Professionals

How To Build Network Marketing Leaders
Volume Two: Activities And Lessons For MLM Leaders

Motivation. Action. Results.
How Network Marketing Leaders Move Their Teams

What Smart Sponsors Do
Supercharge Our Network Marketing Team

More books...

Why You Need to Start Network Marketing
How to Remove Risk and Have a Better Life

How To Build Your Network Marketing Nutrition Business Fast

How Speakers, Trainers, and Coaches Get More Bookings
12 Ways to Flood Our Calendars with Paid Events

How To Build Your Network Marketing Utilities Business Fast

Getting "Yes" Decisions
What insurance agents and financial advisors can say to clients

Public Speaking Magic
Success and Confidence in the First 20 Seconds

Worthless Sponsor Jokes
Network Marketing Humor

ABOUT THE AUTHORS

Keith Schreiter has 30+ years of experience in network marketing and MLM. He shows network marketers how to use simple systems to build a stable and growing business.

So, do you need more prospects? Do you need your prospects to commit instead of stalling? Want to know how to engage and keep your group active? If these are the types of skills you would like to master, you will enjoy his "how-to" style.

Keith speaks and trains in the U.S., Canada, and Europe.

Tom "Big Al" Schreiter has 50+ years of experience in network marketing and MLM. As the author of the original "Big Al" training books in the late '70s, he has continued to speak in over 80 countries on using the exact words and phrases to get prospects to open up their minds and say "YES."

His passion is marketing ideas, marketing campaigns, and how to speak to the subconscious mind in simplified, practical ways. He is always looking for case studies of incredible marketing campaigns that give usable lessons.

As the author of numerous audio trainings, Tom is a favorite speaker at company conventions and regional events.

Printed in Great Britain
by Amazon

83390413R00068